DOGS SET X

WHIPPETS

Megan M. Gunderson
ABDO Publishing Company

visit us at
www.abdopublishing.com

Printed in the United States of America, North Mankato, Minnesota.
102012
012013

 PRINTED ON RECYCLED PAPER

Cover Photo: Alamy
Interior Photos: Alamy p. 13; Getty Images pp. 5, 7, 9, 11, 15, 19; iStockphoto pp. 16–17;
    Thinkstock p. 21

Editors: Rochelle Baltzer, Tamara L. Britton
Art Direction: Neil Klinepier

Cataloging-in-Publication Data

Gunderson, Megan M., 1981-
 Whippets / Megan M. Gunderson.
   p. cm. -- (Dogs)
Includes bibliographical references and index.
ISBN 978-1-61783-593-3
1. Whippet--Juvenile literature. 2. Dogs--Juvenile literature. I. Title.
636.753--dc23
                                                        2012946336

CONTENTS

The Dog Family 4

Whippets 6

What They're Like 8

Coat and Color. 10

Size 12

Care 14

Feeding 16

Things They Need 18

Puppies 20

Glossary 22

Web Sites. 23

Index. 24

THE DOG FAMILY

Around the world, dogs are guards, companions, herders, and guides. They have worked closely with humans for 12,000 years. Today, there are more than 78 million pet dogs in the United States alone.

All dogs belong to the family **Canidae**. Scientists believe they descended from the gray wolf. These wolves are part of the same animal family.

Dogs have excellent senses of sight and smell. Originally, humans relied on dogs for these skills when hunting. Over time, humans **bred** dogs for many different jobs.

Some dogs were bred for speed. Others were bred to be protectors or to keep people company at home. Whippets are stars in all three areas. They are excellent racers, watchdogs, and companions.

A dictionary from 1550
defines the word whippet as
"a lively young woman."

WHIPPETS

Whippets are sight hounds. They were **bred** for speed, **stamina**, and grace. This helped them excel at chasing and capturing small game. Whippets may descend from greyhounds, Airedales, Yorkshire terriers, and several other breeds.

Whippets were originally called "snap-dogs." They got this name from snapping up the most rabbits during **coursing** competitions.

Then, whippets became popular racing dogs. English mill operators living in Massachusetts first brought the breed to the United States. This area became the nation's center of whippet racing.

Whippets and other sight hounds chase their prey by sight. These dogs excel at racing and tracking events.

The **American Kennel Club (AKC)** recognized the whippet in 1881. The **breed** is part of the AKC's hound group. Other breeds in this group include the beagle, the dachshund, and the Irish wolfhound.

What They're Like

Whippets are known for their speed. They can fly by at 35 miles per hour (56 km/h)! These athletic dogs are curious, too. That means they may run off to investigate something that catches their interest.

These graceful dogs make excellent companions. They are quiet and gentle. And, they are loyal and affectionate with their owners. They will snuggle on your lap or in your bed!

Whippets are natural hunters. So, not all whippets do well with small animals. But, most are good with children and other dogs.

Whippets are generally quiet. These excellent watchdogs will only bark when necessary.

COAT AND COLOR

Whippets have short, smooth coats. Pet a whippet and its coat will feel firm. However, a short coat means a whippet's thin skin can be easily damaged. Take special care when your whippet is running outside.

Whippet owners have their pick of a wide variety of coat colors. This **breed** features black, blue, **fawn**, red, **sable**, tan, and white coats. Other options are **brindle** or black and white.

A whippet's eye color depends on its coat color. The eyes range from dark brown to nearly black. The whippet's nose should be a solid color. It can be black, dark blue, or dark brown.

Whippets love the sun! In fact, consider putting sunscreen on your dog's nose, ears, and belly.

SIZE

Whippets are medium-sized dogs. Males stand 19 to 22 inches (48 to 56 cm) tall at the shoulders. Females are slightly smaller. They measure 18 to 21 inches (46 to 53 cm) high. Males can weigh up to 35 pounds (16 kg). Females may weigh as little as 20 pounds (9 kg).

This elegant **breed** features a naturally arched back. The whippet has straight front legs and powerful back legs. Its feet have hard, thick pads and long toes. Its long, tapered tail curves upward.

The whippet's neck is long and muscular. The head features large, round to oval eyes. The long, strong **muzzle** covers bright white teeth. All together, these features give the whippet a keen, intelligent expression.

The whippet's small ears are folded, even when the dog is on alert.

CARE

Your whippet needs regular exercise. Taking walks and playing with your dog will help you stay in shape, too! Just be sure these speedy dogs play in safe, fenced areas.

Whippets are easy to care for. Their short coats require little grooming. A rubber pad or grooming glove will help remove dead hair and dirt. A **chamois** will make the coat shine.

Bathe your whippet when it's dirty using a shampoo made for dogs. Whippets get cold easily. So be sure to keep them warm and dry after a bath.

Regular visits to the veterinarian are a must. The veterinarian will provide necessary **vaccines** for your pet. And, he or she can **spay** or **neuter** whippets that are not going to be **bred**.

Your pet will love running and playing with other whippets.

FEEDING

There are lots of options when it comes to feeding your dog. Commercial dog foods may be dry, semimoist, or canned. Read the label when choosing one. It should say "complete and balanced." And, meat or fish should be listed as one of the first ingredients.

Talk to your veterinarian about the proper amount of food for your whippet. Being overweight is harmful to an adult dog's health and life span. And, it can hurt a growing puppy's bones.

Puppies should get three or more small meals a day. Their little stomachs can't handle too much food at once! Adult whippets can eat one meal in the morning and one at night. Fresh water should be available at all times.

Put your whippet's food and water in stainless steel bowls. These are easy to clean. And unlike plastic bowls, puppies can't chew them up!

Avoid feeding your whippet people food. Some of it is not safe for dogs. And, extra treats can lead to begging.

THINGS THEY NEED

Your whippet may enjoy snuggling in your bed. But, it should have a bed of its own. Provide a crate with soft bedding. This gives your pet a safe, cozy place to relax.

Toys will help keep your whippet entertained. Puppies especially need something to chew on. Distract them from your belongings with safe chew toys.

A curious whippet may run off in a flash. So be sure to use a sturdy leash and a lightweight nylon collar. If your dog does escape, license and identification tags will help it get returned to you.

Remember, whippets get cold easily. So be sure to dress your pet in a sweater during cold weather.

PUPPIES

Mother dogs are **pregnant** for about 63 days. Whippets usually have five to seven puppies per **litter**. Puppies are born blind and deaf. They can see and hear after two to three weeks. Around the same time, puppies begin walking, barking, and wagging their tails.

If you decide the whippet is the perfect **breed** for you, find a good breeder. He or she may put you on a waiting list.

Your puppy should come from a clean home. There, take time to meet your puppy's mother. She should have a good temperament. Also be sure your puppy has healthy skin, clear eyes, and clean ears.

Whippet puppies have lots of energy! They need to be trained so they become well-behaved dogs.

Socialize your whippet and provide it with a safe home. It will be a loving companion for the next 14 years.

A good breeder will tell you which vaccines your puppy has already had and which it will soon need.

GLOSSARY

American Kennel Club (AKC) - an organization that studies and promotes interest in purebred dogs.

breed - a group of animals sharing the same ancestors and appearance. A breeder is a person who raises animals. Raising animals is often called breeding them.

brindle - having dark streaks or spots on a gray, tan, or tawny background.

Canidae (KAN-uh-dee) - the scientific Latin name for the dog family. Members of this family are called canids. They include wolves, jackals, foxes, coyotes, and domestic dogs.

chamois (SHA-mee) - a soft, bendable leather or cloth.

coursing - using dogs to chase game by sight.

fawn - a light grayish brown color.

litter - all of the puppies born at one time to a mother dog.

muzzle - an animal's nose and jaws.

neuter (NOO-tuhr) - to remove a male animal's reproductive glands.

pregnant - having one or more babies growing within the body.

sable - having black-tipped hairs on a silver, gold, gray, fawn, or brown background.

socialize - to adapt an animal to behaving properly around people or other animals in various settings.

spay - to remove a female animal's reproductive organs.

stamina - the power to endure fatigue, disease, or hardship.

vaccine (vak-SEEN) - a shot given to prevent illness or disease.

WEB SITES

To learn more about whippets, visit ABDO Publishing Company online. Web sites about whippets are featured on our Book Links page. These links are routinely monitored and updated to provide the most current information available.

www.abdopublishing.com

INDEX

A
adoption 20
American Kennel Club 7

B
bed 18
body 12
breeder 20

C
Canidae (family) 4
character 4, 6, 8, 12, 18, 20, 21
coat 10, 14
collar 18
color 10
competitions 4, 6
crate 18

E
ears 20
exercise 14
eyes 10, 12, 20

F
feet 12
food 16, 17

G
grooming 14
guarding 4

H
head 12
health 10, 16, 20
history 4, 6, 7
hunting 4, 6, 8

L
leash 18
legs 12
license 18
life span 16, 21

M
muzzle 12

N
neuter 14
nose 10

P
puppies 16, 17, 18, 20

R
reproduction 20

S
senses 4, 20
sight hounds 6
size 12, 16
skin 10, 20
socializing 21
spay 14
speed 4, 6, 8, 14, 18

T
tail 12, 20
teeth 12
toys 18
training 20

U
United States 4, 6

V
vaccines 14
veterinarian 14, 16

W
water 17